Austin Phelps

The Relations of the Bible to the Civilization of the Future

Austin Phelps

The Relations of the Bible to the Civilization of the Future

ISBN/EAN: 9783337100445

Printed in Europe, USA, Canada, Australia, Japan

Cover: Foto ©Lupo / pixelio.de

More available books at **www.hansebooks.com**

The relations of the Bible to the Civilization of the Future.

A

SERMON

DELIVERED BEFORE

IS EXCELLENCY NATHANIEL P. BANKS,

GOVERNOR,

HIS HONOR ELIPHALET TRASK,

LIEUT. GOVERNOR,

The Honorable Council,

AND

THE LEGISLATURE OF MASSACHUSETTS,

AT THE

ANNUAL ELECTION,

WEDNESDAY, JANUARY 2, 1861.

BY

AUSTIN PHELPS,

BARTLET PROFESSOR IN ANDOVER THEOLOGICAL SEMINARY.

BOSTON:
WILLIAM WHITE, PRINTER TO THE STATE.
1861.

The relations of the Bible to the Civilization of the Future.

A

SERMON

DELIVERED BEFORE

HIS EXCELLENCY NATHANIEL P. BANKS,

GOVERNOR,

HIS HONOR ELIPHALET TRASK,

LIEUT. GOVERNOR,

The Honorable Council,

AND

THE LEGISLATURE OF MASSACHUSETTS,

AT THE

ANNUAL ELECTION,

WEDNESDAY, January 2, 1861.

BY

AUSTIN PHELPS,

BARTLET PROFESSOR IN ANDOVER THEOLOGICAL SEMINARY.

BOSTON:
WILLIAM WHITE, PRINTER TO THE STATE.
1861.

Commonwealth of Massachusetts.

In Senate, January 5, 1861.

ORDERED, That a Committee be appointed to present the thanks of the Senate to the Rev. Dr. PHELPS of Andover, for his very able and appropriate Sermon preached before the Government of the Commonwealth on Wednesday last, and to request a copy thereof for the press.

And Messrs. UNDERWOOD, WALKER, and HARDY, are appointed said Committee.

S. N. GIFFORD, *Clerk.*

Commonwealth of Massachusetts.

STATE HOUSE, SENATE CHAMBER, BOSTON,
January 7, 1861.

REV. SIR,—By an Order unanimously passed on the 5th instant, the undersigned were instructed to present to you the thanks of the Senate for the able Sermon preached by you before the Government of the Commonwealth on the 2d inst., and to request a copy of the same for the press.

Be assured, Sir, it affords us sincere pleasure to communicate to you a tribute so well deserved, and we trust it will be both agreeable and convenient for you to furnish to the Senate a copy of the Sermon for the press as solicited, at an early day.

> M. S. UNDERWOOD,
> FREEMAN WALKER,
> ALPHEUS HARDY,
> *Committee of the Senate.*

Rev. Dr. AUSTIN PHELPS, Andover, Mass.

ANDOVER, MASS., January, 8, 1861.

GENTLEMEN,—I have the honor to acknowledge the receipt of your letter of yesterday, communicating to me the wishes of the Senate that a copy of the Sermon, which it was my privilege recently to deliver before the Government of the Commonwealth, be given to the press.

It will give me pleasure to comply with the request, as soon as the manuscript can be made legible to the printer.

Please to accept my cordial acknowledgment of the courtesy with which you have expressed to me the vote of your honorable body, and believe me to be,

> With sentiments of high regard,
> Your ob't serv't,
> AUSTIN PHELPS.

To the Hon. M. S. UNDERWOOD, Hon. FREEMAN WALKER, Hon. ALPHEUS HARDY, Committee of the Senate of Massachusetts.

Commonwealth of Massachusetts.

IN SENATE, January 15, 1861.

The Committee to which was committed the Order of the 5th inst. have attended to the duties prescribed in the Order, and have received from the Rev. Dr. PHELPS a manuscript copy of his Sermon preached before the Government of the Commonwealth on the 2d inst., which together with the correspondence is herewith laid before the Senate, and your Committee report the accompanying Order.

For the Committee,

M. S. UNDERWOOD, *Chairman.*

Accepted.   S. N. GIFFORD, *Clerk.*

IN SENATE, January 15, 1861.

ORDERED, That eight thousand copies of the Election Sermon preached by the Rev. Dr. AUSTIN PHELPS, before the Government of the Commonwealth on the 2d inst., be printed for the use of the Legislature.

S. N. GIFFORD, *Clerk.*

SERMON.

PSALMS CXIX. 99, 100.

I HAVE MORE UNDERSTANDING THAN ALL MY TEACHERS: FOR THY TESTIMONIES
ARE MY MEDITATION. I UNDERSTAND MORE THAN THE ANCIENTS, BECAUSE I
KEEP THY PRECEPTS.

The custom which we honor in the services of this day, has come down to us from an ancestry, whom history has learned to recognize among the civilizing powers of the world. Their power is, for the most part, latent, like the forces of nature. Like those, also, it is constructive. It has been working now for two centuries and more; yet, to-day, it is going on with its creations, giving birth to States, fashioning institutions, breathing free life into nations, with the same unconsciousness of its own majesty which belongs to gravitation.

Like all such unconscious forces in the moral world, however, it is not the power of the men who represented it, but of certain principles which were *in* the men. Those principles, as related to the progress of civilization, may be reduced to two, of a very simple character. The one is, their faith in the Word of God; the other, their faith in the world's future.

2

Our Fathers had faith in the Bible. They believed it as no abstraction, concerned rather with other worlds than with this. They embraced it as the most intense reality they knew of; as necessary to their daily welfare as the daily sunrise. They grounded their domestic, and literary and civil institutions upon it, no less heartily than their churches, and creeds, and pulpits. They would have put a man in the pillory who should have so insulted their consciences, and expressed the degradation of his own, as to deny the obligation of a State to conform to the same standard of right with that which should govern the individual. They consulted the ministers of religion in the framing of their statutes, at the very time when their care against priestly domination was so vigilant, that they forbade the clergy to solemnize the right of marriage. They fought the battles of the State, with Bibles in their knapsacks. They expounded the institutes of Moses, and sung the Psalms of David, on the eve of their victories. It was their faith in the Word of God which moved that Act of the American Congress, by which, at the height of the Revolution, side by side with appropriations for the purchase of gunpowder, there stood an Order for the importation of twenty thousand copies of the Scriptures.

From such a faith as this, it was an inevitable corollary that our fathers should have faith also in the future destiny of this world. Such men could not believe that God would abandon the nations. They

were stern predestinarians; but theirs was faith in the
predestined triumph of right over wrong, of truth over
falsehood, of liberty over slavery, and of a Christian
civilization, therefore, over barbarism, however rooted
in history. If ever men deserved the title, they were
Men of the Future. Their ideas penetrated into
coming times farther than they themselves saw. They
were the builders of structures, of which they were not
consciously the architects. It has been well said of
them, that they had a " high constructive *instinct*, raising them above their age, and above themselves."
Men who are raised above their age, and above themselves, by whatever power, have great visions of truth,
which suggest, when they do not reveal, a great future.
It was a spiritual inheritance from such men which
moved John Adams, in the Congress of 1775, to say,
" No assembly ever had a greater number of great
objects before them. Provinces, nations, empires, are
small things before us." *

Tracing our institutions to their origin in such an
ancestry, we may not unfitly regard it as our birth-
right to consider, on an occasion like this:

SOME OF THE RELATIONS OF THE BIBLE TO THE CIVILIZATION
OF THE FUTURE.

The discussion of this theme here must necessarily
be fragmentary. It will be my object to direct your
thoughts to a few only, of the facts in which lie the

---

* Life and Works of John Adams, vol. i., p. 170.

germs of the control which the Scriptures must exert over the progress of mankind.

I. Of these, we may observe in the first place, that the Scriptures contain the most ancient forms of truth now known to men. In any enlarged view of the forces which civilize communities, a place must be found for the instinctive reverence of the human mind for antiquity. A thing is presumptively true if it is old; and an old truth men *will* revere. Such is human nature. We all have historic feelers, which reach out into the past, for something to lay hold of, and to hold on by, in the rush of things around us. He is not a bold man, but a weak one, rather, who can tear himself absolutely loose from those roots which run into the under-ground of other ages. It would be an irreparable loss to the civilizing forces of Christendom, if the faith of the Christian world could be destroyed in the descent of the race from one pair; so ennobling and so stimulating to culture is this instinct of reverence for a long-lived unity. Especially is its power felt in the fashioning and perpetuating of civil and social institutions. An institution becomes to a nation like an heirloom to a family; the longer it *has* been, the more worthy *to be* it appears to the nation's heart. England, within a century, has borne shocks of her social framework which no other nation in Europe could have survived, in part because she has a thousand years of history.

With all the abuses to which this susceptibility of
our nature is liable, it is in our nature, and for wise
purposes. Within its normal limits, and kept in
balance by the opposite spirit of inquiry, its operation
is healthful. No grand elevation of society is ever
attained without its aid. The Bible invites a large
and free indulgence of it, by the fact that, in this
volume are contained the earliest truthful thoughts of
our race, in written forms.

To give definiteness to this view, let several specifi-
cations be observed in its illustration. It is, for instance, a fact, the significance of which Infidelity
appreciates, if we do not, that the only authentic *history* of the world before the Flood, is found in the
sacred books of Christianity. The world of the future
never can know any thing of the Antediluvians, except
from the Jewish historian. It would be worth centuries of toil to the socialism of Europe, if the infidel
science on which it is founded could blot out this one
fact in the relations of the world to the Pentateuch.
We have also, in the books of Moses,—what no other
literature can show—one or two stanzas of poetry,
which were actually composed in the antediluvian
infancy of the race. Does it not help us to some conception of the venerableness of these volumes, to recall
that they were written eleven hundred years before
Herodotus, whom all other literature denominates the
father of history? The Hebrew jurisprudence is seven
hundred years older than that of Lycurgus, and two.

thousand years older than that of Justinian. You
have heard that Thomas Jefferson was indebted for
his conception of our American Government, to the
polity of an obscure Calvinistic church in Virginia.
But Republicanism was foreshadowed in the Hebrew
Commonwealth, three thousand years before the settle-
ment of Jamestown.

Dr. Johnson once read a manuscript copy of the
book of Ruth, to a fashionable circle in London.
They begged to know of him, where he obtained such
an inimitable pastoral. What would have been their
amazement, if he had concealed the fact of the inspired origin of the story, and had told them that it
was an ancient treasure, written twenty-five hundred
years before the discovery of America? The lyric
poetry of the Hebrews was in its golden age, nearly
a thousand years before the birth of Horace. The
author of Ecclesiastes discussed the problem of evil,
six hundred years before Socrates in the dialogues of
Plato; and the epithalamium of the Canticles is a
thousand years older than Ovid. The book of Esther
was a venerable fragment of biography, stranger than
fiction, at least fifteen hundred years old at the dawn
of the romance-literature of Europe. The Proverbs
of Solomon are, by nine hundred years, more ancient
than the treatises of Seneca. The entire bulk of the
prophetic literature of the Hebrews, a literature ex-
traordinary, one which has laws of its own, to which
there is and can be no parallel, in any uninspired

workings of the human mind — this mysterious, often
unfathomable compendium of the world's future, which
the wisdom of twenty centuries has not exhausted, was
the whole of it anterior to the Augustan age of Rome;
and even the writers of the New Testament are, all of
them, of more venerable antiquity than Tacitus, and
Plutarch, and Pliny the younger.

And what shall be said of the book of Job? Biblical scholars can only conjecture its age; but if that
conjecture be true, this is the oldest volume now
existing, at least a thousand years older than Homer.
It was already an ancient poem when Cecrops founded
Athens. When Britain was invaded by the Romans,
it was more time-worn than the name of Julius Cæsar
to-day, is to us. Natural philosophers now turn to
its allusions as the only recorded evidence we have,
of the state of the arts and sciences four thousand
years ago. A living commentator on the book has
collated from it passages illustrative of the then
existing state of knowledge, respecting astronomy,
geography, cosmology, meteorology, mining operations,
precious stones, coining, writing, engraving, medicine,
music, hunting, husbandry, modes of travel, the military art and zoölogy. Any other work, surely, which
should be so fortunate as to be of uninspired authority, and should give to the world the obscurest authentic hints of the state of these sciences and arts
forty centuries back, would be hailed as a treasure
worthy of a nation's purchase.

But these vestiges of antiquity are of little moment, considered merely as curiosities of literature. The thing which gives them claim to notice at the present is, that through them there runs a chain of truth, representing a work of God for this world's welfare, and that this is the only thing in the world's history which goes back, in authentic record, to the beginning of time. Such a volume must be, sooner or later, a power in the world's enlightenment, if for no other reason, for the strength of its appeal to man's reverence for long-lived truth. Nations cannot forever throw off its authority if they would. Governments cannot permanently seal it up, nor political science treat it with the contempt of silence. Armies cannot trample it out of life in the souls of men. Manly souls will not let it go from them. It must be felt as one of the powers of control on earth, if this clinging of our nature to ancient forms of truth is designed, in God's purposes, to hold the world fast to any thing in the evolution of its destiny.

II.* The Sovereignty of the Scriptures in the progress of mankind is further suggested by the fact, that they contain the only development of Oriental mind, which can be an authority in the civilization of the

* In consequence of the lateness of the hour at which the services commenced, this division of the Discourse, and several other paragraphs, were omitted in the delivery.

future.   In an estimate, on any large scale, of the probable advancement of our race, it is impossible to leave
out of account the immense masses of being which are
congregated in the East.   If the most recent reckonings
of the population of the globe are true, considerably
more than the half of mankind are east of the Mediterranean.   Oriental scholars tell us that they find
there a civilization as complicated, and in its kind as
perfect, as that of the West.   Recent history indi-
cates a probable design of Providence, to bring the
two types of humanity into contact, it may be for
a time into conflict, with each other.   The western
mind is reaching out from Europe overland, and from
this continent across the Pacific, and from both it is
peering around the Capes, to find out the resources of
that Asiatic world, and if possible, to use them.
Every thing betokens an approach of these ends of
the earth to greet each other.   But for what purpose
is the greeting, as it regards that oriental half of mankind?   What type of the Asiatic mind, other than
that found in the Scriptures, has any prospect of
impressing itself on the world's future?   What other
can possibly become a vitalizing agency, in the progress of any thing that enters into our ideal of an
elevated and refined humanity?

It is a fact of which we are apt to be oblivious, in
responding to questions of this kind, that all the
ascendant forces working in modern civilization are
occidental.   They are the offspring, immediately, of the

3

western races, of western ideals of taste, of manners, of learning, of arts, of commerce, of government, and of religion. The national temperaments which they represent, the histories which lie back of them, and the languages which express them, are all the growth of western climes. The old fancy that empire follows the sun, is sober truth in the annals of civilization. Oriental life has no perceptible power in them as an authority, in any other development than that found in the Scriptures. With the exception of a small group of scholars given to Asiatic researches, the circle even of scholarly thought, in our day, does not go back of the Greek literature chronologically, nor eastward of it geographically. The ancient seats of power have no lines of telegraph connecting them, in the conceptions of modern scholarship, with the empires of the West. The connection exists historically, but it is handed over to antiquarians. Who thinks of it, often, in observing the growth of manhood on this side of the Atlantic? To whom is our derivation from Asiatic progenitors any thing more than a curiosity in ethnologic history? What is there existing in the oriental forms of life to remind us of it? Where are the powers of eastern thought, which are now creating any thing that seems worthy of the regard of an American scholar or statesman? What have we learned from the Japanese embassy, that has seemed worthy to be engrafted upon American life and manners? Where are the great libraries of the

East? where are the universities? where are the men of literary renown, to attract literary travel beyond the Bosphorus? Where are the advanced forms of government, the improved ideas of liberty, the superior systems of jurisprudence, the more perfect balancing of the social forces, which should lead an American senator to seek out the wise men of the East? Where is there any thing eastern, which is now projecting itself, by the energy of its own merits, upon western civilization? The truth is, that a new world has sprung up westward of the Euphrates and the Ural mountains, which is more than newly discovered continents. Occidental *mind* is a novelty, as related to the earlier developments of the race. It is almost as much isolated from its oriental progenitors, at all those points of sympathy which form inlets of influence, as if it were the mind of another planet. The only volume, the only thing of elemental energy, which forms an isthmus between the two, on any large scale, is the Christian Scriptures. These have affinities for both. Through these they can come together in brotherhood.

Suspending now, for a few moments, the observation of this fact, let it be remarked, on the other hand, that the oriental development of man, as a whole, is giving no signs of having finished its work in the Divine plans respecting the world's progress. The oriental races are not only the grandest in respect of numbers, but they are the most various in respect of character, which this planet has yet borne. It is not probable that they are to be a blank in the civilization of the future. Is it not to the last degree improbable, that imbecility is to settle henceforth upon that immense oriental brain? He must have a singular theory of the ascendency of races, who can persuade himself that our culture, so exlusively occidental as it is, has received all that it can receive from that ancient stock. Nothing in the Divine methods of working gives countenance to such presumption.

What *is* the law of Providence, respecting nations and races, which have finished their work as Powers in the world's destiny? It is the law of dissolution. When a nation has ended its mission, in the evolutions of the drama which Providence is enacting, that nation dies. When a race of men has reached the point at which God has no farther use for them, in the future moulding of nations, that race goes out of being as a visibly distinct stock of manhood. It decays and falls off, or by revolution it is pruned off from the trunk, and the sap of the root flows elsewhere. When a type of civilization has grown obsolete in its relations to God's plans for the future, that civilization caves in, and is swallowed up, and covered over by something younger and better. God lives—we may say it reverently— God lives, in his government of this world, for the future, never for the past. Races, nations states, churches, civil institutions, even families—any thing, in short, that would live—must move abreast with Providence.

Christianity, which, as wrought into organic social forms, is but the flower and the fruitage of Providence, has always been prophetic in its instincts. It has always been animated with the soul of a seer. It has looked to coming generations, and lived for them. It has never bound itself to the soil, anywhere. It has refused to be hemmed in by geographical lines. It calls no land holy, merely because it was born there. It has no such romance in its make. The law of its being is, that it shall pass away from superannuated to youthful races; from decaying to germinant nations; from expiring to nascent languages. By the decree of God, it is fore-ordained to take possession always of the lands of promise. Its affinities are such as always to draw to itself those elements in families, in churches, in civil institutions, in states, in nations, in tongues, in races of men, which are elastic and eager and foreseeing. Any stock of humanity which is so far worn out, as to have lost, beyond recovery, this capacity for future use, Christianity parts with, leaps away from, and leaves to die. It goes where it finds the most healthy, exuberant energy of production. Mere susceptibility of being acted upon, is not sufficient to preserve a nation, under this law of Providence. It must have power to *do*, either

latent or developed, as well as to *be ;* otherwise its
permission to be is revoked. Nothing in God's plan
of things is purely receptive. Every thing must help
another thing. Any thing dies when it ceases to be
helpful.

Under this law, the entire oriental stock of mind,
if it has finished its work in God's plan, ought now
to be evincing signs of dissolution. The oriental
type of civilization ought, as a whole, to be approaching its extinction. Yet this is by no means the case
with it. The nations which represent it, as a whole
are not dying out. They are not visibly *approaching*
their end. More than one of the Asiatic races seem
to be yet as full-blooded and as virile in their
physical make, and as likely to endure for thirty
generations to come, as they did a thousand years
ago. That ancient development of manhood,
which began on the plains of Shinar, bids fair to
live, by the side of its occidental rival, even if it
does not outlive this, by reason of its calmer flow
of life. If it does thus live, all analogy should lead
us to believe that there is something in it which
deserves to live. There is something in it which
Providence has a use for in the future. It has
energy; it has resources; it has manly tastes and
proclivities; it has something or other, which, under
divine regeneration, would be, will be, a cause of
growth, if infused into the life-blood of the western
races. The circle of occidental development may

be enlarged by it. The channel in which our
civilization is moving, may be thus widened and
deepened.

Resuming now, the connection of this train of
thought with the theme more immediately before us,
let it be repeated, that the only method by which
the oriental mind can ever thus again affect the
civilization of the West, is through the forces of the
Bible. There is nothing at present in oriental ideas
of art, or of commerce, or of government, which can
ever be a power, by the side of the laws, the commerce, the arts of western life. These things, for
the most part, we have to give, not to receive. The
oriental power in the future, must be the production
of the religion of the Bible, re-established in its
ancient seats, and transfused through the forms of
national life there. If new systems of thought are
to grow up among the Asiatics, with any function
of control in the world, they must be the creations
of the Bible. Nothing else represents the oriental
mind, in any form which can ever rouse it to its utmost
of capacity. Nothing else, therefore, can ever enable
it to become a power in the future civilization. None
but a visionary can look for a rejuvenescence of Asia
in the coming ages, from any internal forces now
acting there, independently of the Scriptures. The
history of the East contains nothing which can ever
be to the world, what the revived civilizations of

Greece and Rome were to the middle ages of Europe. Whatever that immense territory has to contribute to the civilization of the future, must come as the illustration of scriptural modes of thought, and as the fruit of scriptural ideas of truth.

Is it visionary to look for this, as one of the results of the infusion of European mind, now going on, in western and central Asia? What, indeed, may not be hoped for from the contact of western with eastern thought, pioneered as the western mind is by Christian missionaries, and pervaded as it is so largely by Christian ideas of life? What a difference would have been created in the destinies of Europe, what centuries of barbarism and conflict, to human view would have been saved, if all that was good in the civilizations of Greece and Rome could have dawned upon the European mind, in Christian, rather than in pagan forms! Yet this, to a very large extent, appears likely to be the process of intellectual and moral and social awakening, to which the vast resources of the Asiatic mind are to be subjected.

Napoleon used to say that the only theatre fit for great exploits was the East. Europe, he said, was contracted. It was provincial. The great races were beyond the Mediterranean. They were in the ancient seats of empire, because the numbers were there. There may be more of truth in this than he meant to utter. The grandest intellectual and moral conquests of the world may yet follow the track of Alexander.

III. Passing now from the oriental world, we may observe a further source of the ascendancy of the Bible in the institutions of the future, in the fact that it is already wrought into all the dominant forces of the civilization of the West. Not that it is in them all with equal efficiency, but in all of them in such degree as to make itself obvious. When we speak of the sway of European and American mind, we speak the conquests of the Scriptures. The elemental ideas of the Bible lie at the foundation of the whole of it. Christianity has wrought such revolutions of opinion; it has thrown into the world so much of original thought; it has organized so many institutions, customs, unwritten laws of life; it has leavened society with such a powerful antiseptic to the putrescent elements of depravity; and it has, therefore, positively created so much of the best material of humanity, that now the noblest type of civilization cannot be conceived of otherwise than as a debtor to the Christian Scriptures.

This obligation becomes most obvious in our modern literature; because there the ideas which are creative in our civilization take on forms of speech. The debt of literature to the Bible is like the debt of vegetation to Light. No other volume has contributed

4

so much to the great organic forms of thought. No other is fusing itself so widely into the standards of libraries. Homer, and Plato, and Aristotle long since gave place to it as an intellectual power. This volume has never yet, at any one time, numbered among its believers a fourth part of the human race; yet it has swayed a greater *amount* of mind, than any other volume the world has known. It has the singular faculty of attracting to itself the thinkers of the world, either as friends or as opponents, always, everywhere. The works of comment upon it, of themselves, form a literature of which any nation might be proud. It is more voluminous than all that remains to us of the Greek and Roman literatures combined. An English antiquarian, who has had the curiosity to number the existing commentaries upon the Scriptures, or upon portions of them, found the number to exceed sixty thousand. Where is another empire of mind to be found like this? Here is a power which, say what we may of its results, has set the Christian world to thinking, and kept it thinking for nearly two thousand years. The unpublished literature of the Christian pulpit surpasses in volume all the libraries of all the nations. " If the sermons preached in our land, during a single year, were all printed," says a living scholar, "they would fill a hundred and twenty million octavo pages. Many of these sermons are, indeed, specimens of human weakness; but the frailest vase may hold roots that will

far outgrow its own dimensions."* The Bible is read
to-day by a larger number of educated minds than any
other book. Innumerable multitudes are poring over
its pages, and are feeling its elevating, refining influence, who never think of it otherwise than as the
authority of their religious faith.† Harvard College,
at a time when the material civilization of Massachusetts was so meagre, that a pewter flagon and a bushel
of corn were received gratefully as a contribution to
the collegiate funds, was founded by men, some of
whom could regale themselves in their hours of lei-
sure, by conversing in the original language of the
Old Testament. Our own language owes, in part, the
very structure it has received to influences exerted
upon it by our English Bible. No Englishman or
American knows well his mother tongue, till he has
learned it in the vocabulary and the idioms of " King
James's Translation." In English form, the Bible
stands at the head of the streams of English conquests; and of English and American colonization
and commerce. It must control, in large degree, the

---

* Prof. E. A. Park's Election Sermon, 1851, page 12.

†" The number of English Bibles and New Testaments, separately,
which have passed through the press, within the recollection of many now
living, has exceeded the number of souls in Britain. In the space of
twelve months, the press has sent forth more than a million of copies, or,
say above nineteen thousand every week, above three thousand every
day, three hundred every hour, or five every minute of working time."—
Anderson's Annals of the English Bible, vol. i., Preface, page 8.

institutions which are to spring up on the banks of those streams, the world over.

It is interesting to observe how the influence of the Bible trickles down into crevices in all other literature, and shows itself at length in golden veins, and precious gems of thought, which are the admiration of all observers, but for which He who made them often receives no thanksgiving.* Shakspeare's conception of woman has been applauded as an absolute original, the creation of no other genius than his. This is not so; it is only a portraiture, in poetic forms, of the Christian ideal of woman, which suffuses with refinement so much of our modern life, and which we owe ultimately to the scriptural doctrine of the atonement. The psalmody of the Scriptures has wrought mightily in the birthnight of more than one revolution for the sake of liberty. The old English and Scottish ballads never exerted on the national mind a tithe of the influence of the Hebrew Psalm. The Commonwealth of England owed its existence, in part, to the psalm-singing

* The late Prof. B. B. Edwards, in his admirable Essay on the Hebrew Poetry, observes: "It supplies the seeds of thought, the suggestive hints, the little germs, the dim conceptions, the outlines of some of the sublimest poems, or passages of poems, to be found in modern literature. It is easy to perceive the influence of the Scriptures on the imagination of Spenser. The Messiah of Pope is only a paraphrase of some passages in Isaiah. The highest strains of Cowper, in his Task, are but an expansion of a chapter of the same prophet. In the Thanatopsis of Bryant, [certain] lines remind us at once of the words of Job. Lord Byron's celebrated Poem on Darkness was evidently founded on a passage in Jeremiah."— Writings, vol. ii., pages 389, 390.

of Cromwell's armies. On the continent of Europe, also, the whole bulk of the despotism of the middle ages went down, for a time, before the rude imitations of the Hebrew psalmody, which were sung in thousands by the people of Germany. The battle-song of Gustavus Adolphus was originally published with this title: " A heart-cheering song of comfort, on the watchword of the Evangelical Army in the battle of Leipsic, September 7, 1631, ' God with us.' "

Who shall worthily portray the obligations of American freedom to the Word of God ? Sir James Mackintosh says that the " Independent divines "— (and it was from them that the clergy of New England were culled)—first taught to John Locke " those principles of religious liberty which they were the first to disclose to the world." *   But why should the Independent *divines* have been the pioneers of such discovery ?   " Democracy is Christ's Government," was the theme of a pamphlet by an humble pastor of Massachusetts, in 1687, which nearly a hundred years later, on the eve of our Revolution, was re-published as a political document becoming to the times.†

---

* Mackintosh's Miscellaneous Works, Second Edition.   London.   Page 152.   In a note upon Orme's Memoirs of Dr. Owen, he adds : " In this very able volume it is clearly proved that the Independents were the first teachers of religious liberty. . . .   It is an important fact in the history of toleration, that Dr. Owen, the Independent, was Dean of Christ church in 1651, when Locke was admitted a member of that College, ' under a *fanatical tutor,*' as Antony Wood says."

† Thornton's " Pulpit of the American Revolution."   Introduction, page 20.

On a Sabbath morning, the 8th of June, 1766, when the old Charter of Massachusetts was in peril, Jonathan Mayhew, pastor of the West Church, in Boston, hallowed his last day of health in this city, by writing to James Otis: " You have heard of the communion of churches. . . . . . While I was thinking of this in my bed, the great use and importance of a communion of colonies appeared to me in a strong light, which led me immediately to set down these hints to transmit to you." * That was the germ from which sprung the Union of these States. But where did Jonathan Mayhew find the idea of the communion of churches? He found it where he found the other great thoughts which inspired his love of liberty. In a sermon preached to his people on the occasion of the repeal of the Stamp Act, he said: " Having learned from the *Holy Scriptures* that wise, and brave, and virtuous men are always friends to liberty, ... and that where the spirit of the Lord is, *there* is liberty; *this* made me conclude that freedom is a great blessing." †

Eloquent defenders of liberty in parliament and senate have echoed the voice of this patriotic pastor, by their own indebtedness to the same fountain of freedom and free speech. The Earl of Chatham

* Bradford's Life of Mayhew. Pages 428, 429.

† " The Snare Broken."—A Thanksgiving Discourse, by Dr. Mayhew, preached May 23, 1766. Page 43.

acknowledged that he owed much of his power in parliamentary debate to the Apostle Paul. Patrick Henry and James Otis were often likened in their day to the Hebrew prophets. Lord Brougham and Daniel Webster have both expressed their sense of obligation to the same models. Webster was for years the concordance of the Senate of the United States. It is said, that some of his ablest opponents have been known to seek the aid of his memory, to furnish them with biblical references, with which to condense and point their own speeches against him. Yet, such was *his* affluence in command of the same resources, that he could afford to give them liberally, and without upbraiding.

To all departments of modern thought, the Scriptures have been what they have been to modern art. It has been said, that the single conception of the Virgin and her Child has achieved more for the elevation of art than all the exhumed models of Greece and Rome. It is a well known fact, that nothing in art itself succeeded in crushing out the moral abominations which many of those models expressed, until the Christian religion flooded the realm of beauty with more intense ideas of life; so that to the purest taste, the Greek Venus has become imbecile by the side of the Christian Madonna. So· is the Bible dropping everywhere its germs of refinement in modern civilization, beyond the depth of Greek and Roman thought in its choicest and most durable forms.

I would not weary you with an enumeration of
examples of a truth so obvious, but it is illustrated
with singular vividness in one phenomenon of our age,
which you will permit me to notice. I allude to the
unconscious debt of infidelity to biblical resources. The
energy of a moral power is often seen most impres-
sively in the disasters which attend its perversions.
So the power with which the Scriptures are working
in modern mind, is disclosed in the vigor of our infidel
literature. That literature owes nearly all the vitality
it has, to its pilferings of Christian nutriment. Its
very life-blood comes by unconscious suction from
Christian fountains. The Pilgrim's Progress and the
Paradise Lost, are not more palpably indebted to the
Bible, than are many of the most thrilling conceptions
in anti-christian productions of our times. The most
popular and effective of them no man could have
written, whose genius had not been developed by
Christianity. No man *would* have written them, whose
infidelity had not been fired by collision with the
epistle to the Romans. Atheism, as is well known,
is now working disastrously among the artisan classes
of Great Britain. But it owes the chief sources of its
power over the popular mind, to the fact that it holds
on to so much of scriptural thought, though strug-
gling to enforce it without a scriptural God. Its
capital ideas are biblical ideas. Strip it of these, and
it would have no more chance of a hearing in the

workshops of Birmingham and Manchester, than the
vagaries of Buddhism.*

Similar to this is the chief lesson, which, in my
view, we have to learn from the life of that misguided
mind, which, for the last twenty years, has been the
prophet of infidelity in this city. I use the term
" infidelity" here, not opprobriously, but as expressing
by common consent the system of opinions which he
held honestly, and which he was too manly to conceal.
He brought to that solitary altar at which he minis-
tered, a scholarship more generous, and a genius more
mercurial, a power of thought more versatile, and a
command of speech more fascinating,—taking him all
in all, a character more earnest, and a life more pure,
than any other of our countrymen has ever arrayed
against those views of truth which *he* was wont to
designate as the "popular theology." For one, I
must concede the vigor of his influence. With all
the evidences which were apparent, that its acme had

* On this topic the learned author of " The Natural History of Enthu-
siasm," remarks as follows : " The *disbelief* of these last days, so far as it
is a scheme of doctrine, may be shown to be a birth of Christian doctrine.
The Atheism partly, and the Theism entirely, of the present time is a
heresy full of Christian sap. By calling it *Christian*, I mean that it has no
meaning at all, except that which it has wrung from elements of Christian
belief, brought into collision one with another. Atheism, in these days, is
not as of old, a metaphysic abstraction, or a cold paradox ; but it is a
living creature, speaking with a loud voice, and showing a ruddy cheek,
because it has drawn life-blood from that which can spare much and yet
live. If the Gospel, the destruction of which is so eagerly desired by
some among us, were actually to breathe its last, not one of the schemes of
doctrine which is now offered to us in its stead would thenceforward draw
another breath."—The Restoration of Belief, page 215.

5

been reached, and its decline had commenced, during the last years of his life, I am compelled to believe that no candid man among his opponents, who knows the classes of mind which have been addressed, and the energy with which they have been moved, in yonder Music Hall, will feel that, as a friend of truth, he can afford to ignore that influence, or to underrate it. We have not yet seen the end of it. The man has gone; but he represented, and his name still represents, opinions which are a power in the conflict of ideas among us. Yet his power was not the power of his infidelity. It was the power of his unconscious obligations to the very truth which he discarded. His great ideas, those by which he roused the popular conscience, and often swayed the popular heart, were Christian ideas. He owed them to the Bible, which, as an authority, he disowned. He derived them from all the living literatures which he mastered, and from which he could not help imbibing streams of Christian thought. He absorbed them from the very atmosphere, which is electric with our biblical civilization. The workings of his mind were in part like respiration, in which a man inhales the pure air which God made for his sustenance, and exhales mephitic vapors. Many of us, I may say with no invidious intent the majority of us, have been compelled to feel that he maligned *our* religion; he ridiculed *our* sacred oracles; he denounced *our* hope of heaven; he scoffed at *our* Redeemer; he uttered language, which, from *our* lips,

would be blasphemy against *our* God. Yet, the internal forces which bore up, as on a ground swell, this
nameless craft so revolting to our view, and propelled
it often at the top of the wave in the popular vision,
were forces, every one of which sprung from that
ocean of inspired thought, whose great deeps were
broken up in the civilization and the literature around
him. His idea of the dignity of manhood, of the
singleness of individual being, of the brotherhood of
the race, of the intensity of life under the shadow of
immortality, of the paternity and the love of God, of
the right of free inquiry, of the despicableness of
cant in every form, and the ideas of social and of
political, and of moral reform, which grew out of these
as corollaries — such were the elements of his strength.
For the right to wield them, he stood up as a free
man, with a free tongue, and for this we honor him.
Yet, for every one of these ideas we hold him as
a debtor to the old Scriptural Theology of New
England.

Thus it is with every development of infidelity,
which has force enough of character to render it
respectable. It feeds on Christianity itself, and grows
lusty *therefore*. Christian thought comes into this
world, and goes through it, like an immense projec-
tile. It creates, in the surrounding atmosphere on
either side, currents which are no part of it. Yet
they imitate its magnitude; they border on its track;
they catch the rate of its momentum, and so keep

pace with it in speed, like the wind of a cannon ball.
Hence it is that infidelity appears often to grow in the
intensity of its spirit.   Hence it seems often to accumulate resources of destructiveness.   Each new phase
of it seems more formidable than the last.   It is
because the scriptural standards of thought are working their way deeper into the convictions of men, and
are spreading wide their influence, and are hastening
to their results in perfected forms of civilization.
The whole being of a Christian nation is thus intensified.   The Bible, like the sun, thus shines on the
evil and on the good.   It fertilizes the soil of infidel
opinions ; and these, in turn, fling up in defiance of it
a portion of the fruits of its own vitality.

IV. Some of the views thus far presented involve
another fact, indicative of the ascendancy of the Bible
in the future progress of the race.   It is, that the
Bible discloses the only groundwork and process of
a perfect civilization, as a practicable result.

A scheme of social advancement, as such, the Bible
does not delineate.   The word 'civilization' does not
once occur in it.   The *things* in which an elevated
social economy reveals itself to political wisdom, are
not at all obtrusive upon the foreground of scriptural
thought.   Wealth, arts, literature, science, urbanity
of manners, domestic comfort, institutions of charity,
free governments, — these are not the salient themes
here, either of argument or of promise.   A reformer

might study pages of this volume, covering a thousand
years of history, and not discover that inspired minds
ever thought of any such sort of thing; yet a wise
man, instructed in God's wisdom, may traverse the
same ground and so discern the gravitating of principles towards social results, as almost to imagine that
inspired minds thought of nothing else.

The idea, out of which the future civilization must
grow, is here, there, everywhere in this Book of Life.
You anticipate me in affirming that that idea is, *the
moral regeneration of the individual.* In this one aim
lies the rudiment of all that is practicable for the
amelioration of the race. This is the germ of the
whole tree. The wisdom of God is to begin at the
beginning. The wise master-builder starts at the
foundation, and builds up. The pulpit, especially in
its friction against more flimsy engines of reform, has
made this idea familiar to us all. Let us therefore
more summarily than would be otherwise desirable,
observe the method by which Christianity works as
an organ of political and social movement.

In the first place, *it exalts spiritual over material
forces.* It aims at souls, rather than bodies. "Mine
is a kingdom," it says, "which is not of this world."
Steam, railways, telegraphs, ships, cotton gins, spin-
ning-jennies, printing presses, and the like, are not in
the Christian theory the elemental civilizing *powers.*
They are effects and incidents. The powers which lie
back of them are ideas. They lay hold of the only

thing on this earth which is immortal. The stir of
physical forces is only the fermentation incident to the
working of ideas in a world of sense. The material
creation groans and travails, because it is put to great
uses in expressing the throes of the spirit which is its
lord. In such a system of things, cotton is not king,
and corn is not king, and gold is not king; thought
is king, mind is king, character is king.

Working thus with spiritual forces, *Christianity
intensifies individual being.* It deals not with humanity but with men, and takes them as they are. It sets
the individual man to searching after God. It stimu-
lates the sense of individual responsibility to a personal
Deity. It evokes the consciousness of individual sin.
It makes a man feel the infinite solitude of guilt, as if
there were no other beings in the universe but himself
and God. To that only Friend it directs his cry for
help, as to One who is not shocked nor disgusted by
his vileness, but who can be touched with the feeling
of his infirmities, and who is ever saying to him,
"Come unto me, my child." It reveals the practicability of individual regeneration by God only, through
individual faith in Christ, expanding and blooming
into the graces of a Christlike character.

Intensifying thus the individuality of the soul,
Christianity presumes the whole process to be, as in
experience it proves itself to be, *a process of symmet-
rical elevation.* An uplifting of the entire being is
the result. Affinities spring into life with all that is

lovely and of good report. Aspirations after growth
in every thing that may dignify a man, come by a law
as sure as that by which respiration comes to the
newly born. Advance becomes a necessity. Heavenly
voices speak, saying, " Come up hither; forget the
things which are behind thee; thine is a high calling."
Lifting thus the individual mind, Christianity *sets
to working a power which is diffusive.* The man is a part
of humanity: he begins to move it, as he himself is
moved. The individual is an elevating force to the
family, and through the family to the community, and
through the community to the state, and through the
state to the age, and the race. Christianity presup-
poses what history proves, that individual consciences,
thus illumined, intensified, redeemed from the dominion of guilt, will sway the world. Dotting the globe
over with points of light, they radiate towards each
other; each reduplicates the illuminating power of
another. They run together, sometimes by imper-
ceptible advances, like the movement of the fixed
stars; yet in golden moments of history, times of re-
freshing to an expectant and weary world, they are
like material light, the swiftest of the elements.
Diffusing itself thus, as a power of moral illumina-
tion, *Christianity is affluent in the production of certain
auxiliary ideas.* These like itself, are spiritual, and
they take on social, and civil, and political forms.
They are constructive ideas. They work in building
institutions, customs, forms and reforms of govern-

ment, much as the instinct in a bee-hive works. From the intensity which the Christian theory of manhood gives to individual being, start forth as collaterals, such ideas as the equality of the race, the brotherhood of man with man, the nobility of woman, the inhumanity of war, the odiousness of slavery, the dignity of labor, the worth of education, and the blessedness of charity. Institutions which are the consolidation of such ideas, Christianity drops from her open hand, in and around the homes of men, for the healing of the nations. And the point of significance is that the nations never get them from any other source.

I have said, that civilization as a scheme of social progress is not expressed in the Bible. Yet, once more, be it observed, that while throwing out into the world these ideas which are auxiliary to its direct aim, the Bible does exhibit, if I may so speak, a certain divine *consciousness, that they must and will, and a purpose that they shall, become constructive elements in society.* This is exhibited, for instance, in that most luminous fact in scriptural history, that God educates nations as the representatives of principles. No thinking man can review the four thousand years of history, covered by the Old Testament, without discerning that nations are servitors of God's purposes, arranged along a line of advance in the development of a plan. They are like a cordon of military posts along a king's highway.

Equally obvious is this breadth of providential design, in the scriptural fact that God destroys some nations to make way for the establishment of truth in others. The biblical interpretation of the history of such empires as those of Babylon and Egypt, is simply this; that when a nation plants itself in the way of a plan of God for the progress of the race, Divine Providence waits with long-suffering, while the pride and pomp and circumstance of national impiety accumulate, but at the same time gathers alongside of these the materials of retribution, and at last, with an awful composure, a composure like to nothing else but the stillness of eternity, God sacrifices that nation to a principle. To any people who are identified with a principle in God's purposes, though they be but a handful of slaves under the task-masters of the Pharaohs, the language of Providence is, " Fear not; since thou wast precious in my sight, thou hast been honorable, and I have loved thee; therefore will I give men for thee, and people for thy life."

The same reach of truth beyond the destiny of the individual, is shadowed forth in certain intimations of biblical writers themselves, that their teachings must become disturbing forces in society. A celebrated English scholar says that the idea of the unnatural structure of the social life of England, in certain respects, first dawned upon his mind in reading the Epistle of James and the prophets of the Old Testa-

6

ment. The commission of our Lord himself to his
disciples, affirms as distinctly as language can, that the
Gospel they were to preach was to become the occasion
of social disquietudes and collisions; and more, that
it was to advance amidst the shock of battle, by
the agency of suffering, and at the cost of life.
" Think not that I am come to send peace on earth,"
is his language, " I come not to send peace, but a
sword."

But we are not left to intimations alone, of the inspired insight into the working of religious ideas in
social institutions.   The *design* of such ideas to work
thus, is seen in some of the actual uses made of them
by inspiration itself.   It is an inexplicable anomaly,
that honest minds can read certain portions of the
Scriptures like some of the teachings of the prophets,
and of the apostle James, and yet hold the scriptural
policy in the applications of the Gospel to social
and political abuses, to be the policy of silence or of
reserve.   The late Dr. Arnold, of Rugby, who perhaps
more than any other man of our times, made the Scriptures his study with reference to this thing, alludes to a
recommendation which had been made in a time of
national commotion in England, that the clergy should
preach only subordination and obedience.   " I seri-
ously say," he writes, " God forbid they should; for
if any earthly thing could ruin Christianity in England, it would be this.   If they read Isaiah and Jeremiah, and Amos and Habbakuk, they will find that

the prophets, in a similar state of society in Judea, did not preach subordination only or chiefly; but they denounced oppression, and amassing overgrown properties, and grinding the laborers to the smallest possible pittance: and they denounced the Jewish high church party for countenancing these iniquities, and prophesying smooth things?"*

The scriptural principle in the application of Christianity to social wrong, may be summed up in this — *the temporary toleration of evil, followed by timely efforts for its extinction.* It is the wisdom of the Bible, as of Providence, to be merciful to the evil and the unthankful. The sufferance of wrong, the toleration of sin even, it endures, so long as the national conscience is not educated to distinct cognizance of the sin. "I have many things to say unto you," is often its sad burden, "but ye cannot bear them now." But, on the other hand, the wisdom of the Bible, as of Providence, is to endure no hiding of wrong, and no compromise with wrong, seen and felt *to be* wrong, by the national mind. When Christian truth has so trained a people, that they begin to rise above the corruption of ages, and to grow into capacity to catch some glimmering of light upon a national distortion, then the prophets and apostles of Christianity are on the alert, quick to point out that distortion as a sin; to denounce it without stint, as a wrong against hu-

* Arnold's Life and Correspondence, American Edition, page 179.

manity, and a crime against God. Then truth becomes
a fire and a hammer. It verifies, by its working, the
saying of one of our wise men; that "when God
prepares a hammer it will not be made of silk." This
is the genius of biblical reform. Large portions of
the Bible are alive with it. Suspense of judgment
upon wrong, I repeat, is in the Scriptures, as it is in
Providence, only so far as it is mercy to the weakness
and the blindness of men. It exists always for the
sake of the extinction of the wrong; never for its
increase, never for its perpetuity, never for the con-
venience of letting it alone. Inspiration does indeed
practice as it preaches the wisdom of the serpent,
but always in conjunction with the innocence of the
dove.

Perhaps more convincingly than in any other form,
the diffusion of the effects of Christianity into the
social economy, is seen in the predictions of the final
triumph of the gospel by the conversion of the world
to Christ. It is impossible to look attentively upon
the scriptural picture of this world as it is to be in its
latter days, without catching from inspiration an as-
surance that those are to be days of great intellectual,
and social, and civil, and political, as well as of moral
elevation. They are to be days of peace among the
nations: swords shall become ploughshares, and spears
pruning hooks. They shall be days of the supremacy
of right over wrong in the government of states. "I
will make thy officers peace, and thine exactors right-

cousness:" "nations shall say, 'come, let us go up to
the mountain of the Lord, and he will teach us of his
ways, and we will walk in his paths.'" They shall
be days in which the great powers of the world shall
acknowledge the dominion of Christ. "All kings
shall fall down before him." It shall be an era of
intellectual advancement. "Wisdom and knowledge
shall be the stability of thy times." * They shall be
times marked by revolutions of false public opinion.
"In that day shall the deaf hear the words of the
book, and the eyes of the blind shall see out of ob-
scurity: they also that erred in spirit shall come to
understanding." Those days shall witness signal advances upon preceding states of society. "For brass
I will bring gold, and for iron silver, and for wood
brass, and for stones iron." The natural obstacles to
progress shall be removed. "Every valley shall be
exalted, and every mountain and hill shall be made
low, and the crooked shall be made straight, and the
rough places plain." Changes so marvellous shall
occur in the relations of conflicting races, that they
shall seem like a reversal of the laws of nature. "The
wolf and the lamb shall feed together; the leopard

* The elder President Edwards, in his History of Redemption, speaking
of the ultimate prevalence of knowledge in the earth, observes: "It may
be hoped that then many of the Negroes and Indians will be divines;
and that excellent books will be published in Africa, in Ethiopia, in Tar-
tary, and other now the most barbarous countries; and not only learned
men, but others of more ordinary education, shall then be very knowing
in religion. Knowledge shall then be very universal among all sorts of
persons." — Works in four Volumes, vol. i., page 481.

shall lie down with the kid; the calf and the young
lion and the fattling together." Is it possible not to
believe that slavery will cease in those days ? " They
shall sit, every man under *his* vine and under *his* fig-
tree, and none shall make them afraid." " The lofti-
ness of man shall be bowed down, and the haughti-
ness of men shall be made low." " Sorrow and sighing
shall flee away." " The voice of weeping shall no
more be heard, nor the voice of crying." " My people
shall dwell in a peaceable habitation, and in sure
dwellings, and in quiet resting-places." " Neither shall
they defile themselves any more with their detestable
things, nor with any of their transgressions."

In no deformed, degraded, brutalized types of
humanity then, but in the noblest and most pure, are
the nations to be given to Christ for His inheritance.
He shall see, — He whose ideal is his own pure consciousness of what manhood *can* be, — *He* shall see of
the travail of His soul, and shall be *satisfied*.

Starting thus with the idea of the moral regeneration of the individual, the word of God conducts us,
by easy and inevitable advances, to that truth which
becomes its own witness to a Christian believer, that
THE CIVILIZATION OF THE FUTURE, AND THE TRIUMPH
OF CHRISTIANITY, ARE IDENTICAL.

This faith was the wisdom of our fathers, in laying
the foundations of New England. Theirs was a hidden
wisdom, which none of the princes of this world knew.

Their ideal of a perfect body politic, was simply that of a *Christian State.* Just two hundred years ago, in the Election Sermon of the year preached by Rev. John Norton, the preacher declared, " That our polity may be compleat according to the Scriptures — this is the very work we engaged for into this wilderness. This is the scope and end of it, that which is written upon the forehead of New England." * " God be thanked," said the fervid pastor of the West Church of Boston, " one may speak freely . . . both of government and religion, and even give some broad hints that he is engaged on the side of liberty, the Bible, and common sense . . . without danger of the Bastile or the Inquisition." † " Liberty, the Bible, and Common Sense! " Thus our wise fathers uttered " broad hints " of the alliance of the great ideas on which their institutions should be built.

And we are here to-day, for what purpose more becoming, than to read anew that writing on the forehead of New England, and interpret it to our children? Surely, never in our history has it been more timely. I should be unworthy to stand in this presence, within these walls from which echo so many voices of the past, beneath the cloud of witnesses who have hallowed this anniversary by their faithfulness, and at

* Thornton's " Pulpit of the American Revolution," page 18.

† Page 2 of Preface to Mayhew's Sermon on the Anniversary of the Death of Charles I., " preached the Lord's Day after the 30th of January, 1749-50."

such' an hour as this in the evolution of our country's
destiny, if I should refuse to accept the application of
the subject we have considered, to the rights and the
duties of the hour.

The details of the crisis which is upon us, need not
be rehearsed here. They have been borne through
the land as by the winds. Have they not seemed at
times to press down the atmosphere to an unnatural
stillness, as if the breath of a nation were stifled by
them? Yet who knows whether or not it has been
the hush which precedes the earthquake? This is
one of those epochs, not infrequent in the history of
great nations, at which God summons them to fall
back upon the principles on which their greatness is
built, and from that point look the future in the eye.
We need to lift up the questions of the hour, above
the strifes of parties, above the frivolities of politics,
above the interests of trade, above the temptations of
ease, and listen for the responses of God's word, with
faith in them as oracles of the future. We need to
weigh events and their probable results, in the spirit
which subdued many of the founders of this republic
to prayer. Said John Adams in 1776: "When I consider the great events which are passed, and those
greater which are rapidly advancing, and that I may
have been instrumental in touching some springs, and
turning some small wheels which have had and will
have such effects, I feel an awe upon my mind which
is not easily described." "In such great changes and

commotions, individuals are but atoms.   It is scarcely
worth while to consider what the consequences will
be to us.   What will be the effects upon present and
future millions, and millions of millions is [the]
question." *   The clear head and the great heart of
a Christian statesman spoke in those words.

Approaching the duties of our time in such a spirit,
we shall ensure the prime virtues of Christian citi-
zenship and Christian legislation.   We shall, in the
first place, *act in the spirit of obedience to constitu-
tional law.*   We have been told, by men whom it has
been an honor to us to respect as our judicial counsel-
lors, that we have enactments on our statute-book,
inconsistent with the compact which binds us to the
sister States of the Confederacy.   *If this be so,* those
enactments will be repealed.   It will be seen that
Massachusetts knows how to do her duty, as well as
to claim her rights.   She will indeed judge leniently
of the passage of such laws, for the genius of Christianity, and the judgment of the Christian world have
taught her in the language of Burke, to "pardon
much to the spirit of liberty."   But she will repeal
those laws, in the faith that liberty can always afford
to be just: and its doom is inevitable if it is built on
a wrong.   It is never pusillanimous to do right.   As
there is always a spot of soft cowardice in the heart

* Life and Works of John Adams, vol. i., pages 219, 199.

7

of a duellist, so is there in the heart of a great people, who dare not retract an error, through fear of *seeming* to fear a threat. But why do I speak thus? A Massachusetts Legislature never yet betrayed the childishness of refusing to hear reason. They are wont, indeed, to be convinced before they act, but once convinced, they need no exhortation from the pulpit or the bench on such a theme as this, to do their duty.

Acting thus in the spirit of Christian statesmanship, we shall *cherish, also, magnanimity towards our misguided brethren.* This is no time to taunt them with their misfortunes; it is no time to upbraid them with their misdeeds. In so grave a crisis, the triumph of a party is unseemly. If the dying prayer of Christ could ever be offered for states deluded to the brink of their own destruction, it is becoming now for our brethren of the South. They surely know not what they do. They misinterpret the word and the Providence of God. They do not hear aright the voices of the future. They are deceived respecting our position in controversy with them. Their press is teeming with falsehoods from northern pens. Up to the limit of national safety, then, we have reason for forbearance. Let the tone of our legislation, and our press, and our pulpits, be generous, until so gentle a virtue is silenced by events. If we can yet be heard in debate, let it be in words of temperance and soberness.

Let us speak at the height of great argum
becoming to Christian states in the discussion of great
principles. If we need a less exalted motive, let us
remember that we can afford to be magnanimous.
For, though, if our brethren suffer, we must suffer
with them, yet what thoughtful man is not appalled
at the imagination of the contrast between their lot
and ours in the last extremity? If there is any truth
in history, if the faith of our fathers has not been
mocking us these two hundred years, if 'liberty' is not

> " A hollow word,
> As if a dead man spake it,"

then surely the Future is ours. No, I will not say
'ours,' except as, through our Christian faith, " all
things are ours, whether things present or things to
come."

Yet not this virtue of forbearance, as I con-
ceive, is the chief of ' the graces' demanded of us in
the present exigency. Regarding the requirements
of the time in the light of a Christian civilization, we
have need to *gird up our fidelity to the principles of
Freedom.* Here lies our chief duty, and our chief
peril. It is useless to blink the fact of the radical
antagonism of elements under the cover of our
national constitution. Two opposing types of civilization are in conflict here, and have been from the
infancy of our Union. The conflict is not one of
physical resources, but of ideas. The strifes of polit-

ical parties have been, as they often are in the history
of great nations, ripples on the surface of affairs.
Underneath, a drifting of the social forces has been
going on, under laws of Providence, as inevitable in
their operations as oceanic currents. It has been
bearing the whole body politic on towards the solu-
tion of the African problem in the civilization of this
continent. Not chiefly is it for the sake of the
African race; it is for the sake of the principles
of civilization which that problem involves. The
statesmen of England now very clearly see that the
American Revolution was the salvation of the liberties of Great Britain, and if of her liberties, then
of all else that is valuable in her institutions. So
the freedom, and if the freedom, the happiness, and
the culture, and the character of every man, woman,
child, of the future generations of America, swing
on the pivot of the African question of to-day. This
is no chimera. It is an illustration of one of the
methods of Providence in the probation of nations.
God tries nations by the conflict of ideas, brought
into conflict in the exigencies of national life. Ideas
of truth and ideas of error are set afloat, and so
long as they float in theories only, they move peace-
ably, because they move asunder. Outside of books,
the world hears very little about them. But
by and by there comes a great practical exigency,
involving the right and wrong of those ideas, and

the nation drifts into it like a ship drifting in a gale
into an icefloe, in which her safety depends, under
God, on the strength of her timbers, the discipline
of her crew, and the nerve of her pilot. Who cares
for the icefloe, as a thing of dispute between the
North Pole and the Equator, provided the freight
of human life can get safely into port? So it is
with these national exigencies. As involving the
questions of sectional rivalry, they are petty. An
earnest man will not look at them. But as tests
of conflicting ideas of civilization, an earnest man
cannot help looking at them. The nation's future
dates from them. A nation's capacity for every thing
that a great people should aspire to, is either
expanded or contracted by them. Not a thing, not
a thought, which a wise, free people ever fought for,
or a Christian people ever prayed for, is outside
of the bearings of such crises. The trial by jury,
the freedom of the press, the rights of commerce,
the sacredness of constitutions, the interests of learning, the integrity of the pulpit, a free Bible, free
worship, free homes—every thing, in short, around
which the battles of Christian liberty have surged
in the past, is put to the hazard in such emergen-
cies ; and the privilege of a people to *have* these
blessings is made to hinge upon their will to *keep*
them, by contending for the ideas which gave them
birth.

National progress and national decline go on visibly from exigence to exigence; not by quiet and easy gradations, in which there is no trial of a people's faith in truth and in God. The immediate occasion of such conflicts of ideas may be insignificant. The abduction of a Jew boy may seem to convulse a continent; so may a tax of three pence on a pound of tea. Be the occasion what it may, when such a conflict comes, it is neither statesmanship nor manliness to evade it by the sacrifice of a principle, or the surrender of a right. Compromise of things not vital may, and may not, be expedient, but beyond that, 'compromise' is a perilous word with which to familiarize the lips of a free people. It should be met as the wary citizens of Boston met the insidious propositions of Bernard, by which he attempted to beguile them into an acceptance of the Stamp Act. "There is a snake in the grass," said they; "we choose Samuel Adams to speak our minds."

Just this, then, I must believe, is the mission of New England at the present juncture of our affairs; it is to stand with temperate, but firm resolve, by the hereditary ideas of liberty, which have become historic among us, and which, under the good Providence of God, have made New England what she is. We owe this to the future of the South, no less than to our own. When such perils to freedom are darkening the air, we can see no points of compass. The blackness falls on the whole land.

From the origin of our government, the influence
of New England has been pre-eminently the influence
of her moral ideas.   These have given the purchase
to the lever, with which she has borne her share
of the lift in national affairs.   We have been accustomed to ground our own liberties on principles
of right—never on devices of expediency.   We have
claimed those liberties; never, at any human tribu-
nal, have we asked for them.   On the same principle,
we have advocated the liberties of other men.   Our
pulpits, our bar, our press, our platforms, our halls
of legislation, our seminaries of learning, have spoken
our love of liberty everywhere for all men, as a
right founded on the laws of God.   Our notions of
freedom and of conscience have thus been welded
together in our history.   " Is it *right*," inquired James
Otis, " to enslave a man because his color is black, or
his . hair short and curled like wool, instead of
Christian hair?"   And that has been the blunt
question of New England from that day to this.   We
have no novel ideas of liberty.   We have no imprac-
ticable theories.   *We stand, on this subject, where we
were born.*   We have proved the practicability of
our theory by the working of our own institutions.
The world knows this.   The world knows, too,
that, as a people, we have not been accustomed
to compromise our views of right for the sake
of our material interests.   God forbid that we
should do it now!   Two hundred and forty years

ago, our fathers buried the thought of such compromise as that; and generations have tramped over
its grave.   It is not for us to call the dead thing to
life again.

But, in giving an irrevocable negative to such
dishonor, it becomes us to count the heaviest cost.
No man can foresee the immediate issue of our
affairs. We are advancing in the dark. We are all
sensible of this. It would be folly to predict the
intelligence of to-morrow's telegraph. But it is not
the usual way of Divine Providence, in the treatment
of gigantic evils, which block up the course of
Christian ideas, and are organized in social institutions, to bring them to an end by bloodless revolutions alone. They do not commonly die of sheer
old age, and go out of sight tranquilly. The decisive
conflict of a Christian civilization with them may be
deferred, but, sooner or later, it must come; and
whenever it comes, they are apt to die as they have
lived,—by violence. If this should be the result of the
conflict with slavery in this country, we or our
children must suffer from the shock. Be it so. Every
man of us should be prepared for this. Possibly God
will avert it from us, but what wise man can expect
such a result, or teach his children to expect it?

There are men, indeed, who tell us that the brunt
of the shock will fall first and last, and heaviest, on
New England. We have too much faith in gravitation to believe that; but be it even so. It will not

be the first time that Right has seemed to be worsted
in the battle. We must be prepared to stand in our
lot, whenever and however, the trial of our free institutions shall come upon us. For these we must be
content to go back to the times of "plain living and
high thinking." The world should know that these
institutions are, at all hazards, to be protected. It
shall be done without bravado, but it shall be done
without compromise, and without restriction.

They are to be defended by the majesty of law, by
the culture of the schools, by the instructions of the
pulpit, by the persuasions of the press, by the wisdom
of the bench, by the eloquence of the platform,
and the bar, and the senate, by free thought and free
speech in our streets, and in our homes, and if need
be, by the sacrifice of fortunes, and by the best blood
we have inherited from men who reckoned not *their*
blood too dear a price of the institutions which they
would give to their children.

Prepared thus to do *and* to suffer, we may trustfully
commit the future of this nation to God in prayer.
Prayer will save this country, when it has gone
beyond the reach of legislation. We may cast it
into the infinity of the plans of God, with repose.

> " As a child drops some pebble small
> Down a deep well, and hears it fall,
> Smiling,"

8

so we may entrust the destiny of this people to the depths of His Will. "If thou seest," is His language to us, "if thou seest the oppression of the poor, and violent perverting of judgment and justice, in a province, marvel not at the matter: for He that is higher than the highest regardeth."

The events of the last month have forced back our thoughts to the great men who have left us. We have said, "Would that they were with us now!" I have been reminded of Wordsworth's apostrophe to Milton, in one of England's dark hours during the French Revolution: —

> "Milton ! Thou shouldst be living at this hour.
> England hath need of thee."

So have we said of this one, and of that one, of the men whom we venerate in our country's history. Eternity only can disclose the volume of prayer which, in these few weeks, has gone up from this land to the God of nations, in the petition of the Hebrew lawgiver, "Let the Lord, the God of the spirits of all flesh, set a *man* over [this people] that [they] be not as sheep, which have no shepherd."

Yet, we have taken courage, when we have looked around us, and numbered the men whom the God of our fathers has given us, in whom the manhood of the fathers still lives. Do I not speak the minds of the citizens of Massachusetts, in recognizing as emi-

nent among such men the retiring chief magistrate of
the Commonwealth ?

I am sure, Sir, that I do not exaggerate the feelings
of the good and true men among us, in expressing
their gratitude to the good Providence of God, for
raising you to offices of trust in the midst of them.
He has permitted us to honor you as one of the creations of the ancient institutions of New England.
When those institutions have been reviled, He has
made it our privilege to respond silently, pointing to
the life and character and administration of the Ex-
ecutive at our State Capitol. Our young men have
been stimulated to achievement by your history ; our
old men have been cheered by it, as being in some sort
a proof of the fidelity of their generation.

We count it as a blessing of God upon us, that He
has put it into your heart to appreciate our seminaries of learning of every rank. We bear you witness
that your care for them has been large-hearted and
impartial. There are youth now in a course of train-
ing in them who will speak to their children, of the
first awakening of high aims in their souls by words
which have fallen from your lips.

The churches and the clergy of the State have
numbered it among the mercies of Providence to this
Commonwealth, that you have been a friend of good
order, of liberty, and of sound morals, and that they
have never feared to see you sitting in the seat of the

scorner. You do not need our praise for these things, but we thank God, on your behalf and ours.

New England has long been accustomed to give up the choicest of her sons to more youthful States. Of such sacrifices Massachusetts has borne her full share. Now that she adds another to the number, may I venture to tell you that she feels a joy for your sake, that you go, as we have been told, to discharge a duty to those who are dependent on your private fortunes. We rejoice in it, as a proof to the world of that which *we* all knew before—which would once have indicated too common a virtue to be spoken of, but a virtue which, in these latter days is beginning to reflect signal honor on a public man—that the Governors of Massachusetts do not understand the meaning of the " *spoils* of office."

We give you, Sir, to the State of your adoption— not unwillingly; for we know where the destinies of this nation are to be decided, and there, we believe, you are needed. But I am assured that I speak the voice of this people when I say, that the *heart* of Massachusetts goes with you. She trusts you to represent her honorably there, as you have done here.

To His Honor, the Lieutenant Governor, and to the Honorable Council, and to you all, Gentlemen of the Legislature, permit me to extend the salutations of the hour—salutations subdued by awe at the grandeur of public duty in times like these. We are approaching a great epoch, if true men are found with wisdom and grace to *make* it great. In you. Massachusetts expects to find such men. She trusts you as the guardians of her honor. She makes you, for the time, the representatives of her conscience. She believes that you will come up to the level of Christian legislation; and that whatever else you part with, you will cling to her ancestral fame, as a State fearing God, obeying Law, "daring to feel the majesty of Right," and loving the liberties of mankind.

www.ingramcontent.com/pod-product-compliance
Lightning Source LLC
Chambersburg PA
CBHW030720110426
42739CB00030B/1013